BOB MANN'S

Automatic Golf Complete

Bob Mann

A FIRESIDE BOOK
Published by Simon & Schuster

New York   London   Toronto   Sydney   Tokyo   Singapore

FIRESIDE
Simon & Schuster Building
Rockefeller Center
1230 Avenue of the Americas
New York, New York 10020

Designed by Caroline Cunningham

Manufactured in the United States of America

10   9   8   7   6   5   4   3   2   1

Library of Congress Cataloging in Publication Data
Mann, Bob.
    [Automatic golf complete]
    Bob Mann's automatic golf complete/Bob Mann.
      p.   cm.
    "A Fireside book."
    An instructional book based on the author's videos.
    1. Golf. I. Title. II. Title: Automatic golf complete.
GV965.M236   1992
796.352—dc20
                                                  92-4539
                                                CIP

ISBN 0-671-74049-0

Contents

Introduction

One of my favorite movies, *The Sting*, was produced by a fellow named Tony Bill. In addition to his film achievements, he is credited with a great Hollywood quote: "A successful producer is a janitor with a good script."

With this in mind, I made a resolution when I began writing golf books and creating video and television programs: I will produce only when I have a valid, fresh message.

This is my third golf book. To bring you fresh material without compromising the simplicity of my Automatic Golf method, I have included information that I know is of interest to a large number of golfers and would-be golfers. This information is based on the many letters I have received and on questions I have been asked during nearly 350 radio interviews.

By reading this book, you will learn not only how my Automatic Golf method will help you produce a great golf swing but you'll also gain an understanding of the mechanics of your newly adopted method.

Players at all levels of skill will be interested in the easy-to-understand chapters in this book describing such things as pre-shot preparation, taking a proper grip, and how to improve your putting and chipping. You'll also benefit from the specific 10-day plan for incorporating my Automatic Golf method into your game. This 10-day plan is brand-new material.

This book also includes all the techniques from my videos, *Automatic Golf—Let's Get Started*, *Automatic Golf—The Method*, and *Son of Automatic Golf—the Specialty Shots*. With this book you're getting the full shot, so tee it high and let it fly.

—Bob Mann

BOB MANN'S

Automatic

Golf

Complete

CHAPTER 1

Why Play Golf?

Eastern philosophies espouse the concept of yin and yang. Yin and yang are the expressions of extremes: dark and light, cold and hot, fast and slow.

In today's modern world, people spend most of their time indoors, in relatively small spaces, surrounded by all sorts of man-made substances. For those caught in the grind of that world, golf is the natural complement. Golf brings us outdoors into nature, the largest of spaces.

Another major attraction of golf is the golfers, who by and large are sociable and straightforward folks. Most golfers have a great sense of humor, and the way most of them swing, a sense of humor is necessary. Being around golfers is one of the most compelling reasons to play the game. Additionally, the career and business contacts that you'll make through golf might open doors for you that might otherwise be padlocked.

Golf is played throughout the world. You'll be able to enjoy it almost everywhere you travel.

Golf is a life-long sport. With reasonable care of your body, you'll be able to play at a decent level well beyond

1-1: Golf is a life-long sport that provides excellent exercise.

the time that you would probably be inclined to "retire" from many other activities.

If you walk around the course, golf is excellent exercise. I recommend carrying a light bag with about seven or eight clubs. If you walk the courses you'll increase your pleasure, your fitness, and play better because your flexibility and circulation will be in a "go" mode throughout the round.

CHAPTER 2

Falling into a Method

The Automatic Golf method might not be available to improve your game were it not for a bicycle.

In 1982 I catapulted over the handlebars of a bike while negotiating a jump on a dirt racecourse. I landed on my right shoulder and ached for weeks.

During my recovery period, I instinctively gravitated to a routine of swinging a golf club several times in a row while gripping it only with my left hand. A few weeks of swinging in this manner taught me more about the essence of a golf swing than I had learned in all my previous years as an amateur and professional golfer.

The first thing I learned by doing this routine was that keeping the club under control during the repetitious swings required a specific placement of my left hand. *Any significant variation of my left-hand grip allowed the club to flop out of control.*

After learning to grip the club properly with my left hand, I was able to add more velocity to the one-handed swing *in direct proportion to the amount of movement of my lower body:* more lower body movement, more swing velocity. Through this process I recognized that a concise

2-1: Practicing your swing while holding the club only with the left hand will give you the "body first, arms and club follow" feeling produced by the Automatic Golf method.

BOB MANN

description of an effective, powerful, and repeating golf swing is: *body first, arms and club follow.* In the proper golf swing the arms and the club simply respond to the lower body move.

By swinging the club while holding it only with my left hand, I realized that the groove we are all seeking for our golf swings is something that occurs automatically because of centrifugal force. Centrifugal force in a golf swing is created only if we utilize the "body first, arms and club follow" method.

This revelation so excited me that I decided to test it on students without delay. I was delighted to find that they too felt and experienced increased power and accuracy with only a minimum of instruction and practice.

CHAPTER 3

Body and Brain: Integration and Interaction

A common medical theory states that the two sides of the brain direct different functions and tasks. The right side of the brain is free-flowing and creative, the left side is methodical and calculating. The right side of the brain controls the left side of the body and, conversely, the left side of the brain controls the right side of the body.

This information is particularly interesting as it applies to golf. For a right-handed player, the left side of the body must be dominant because it pulls the club through the swing.

From this factor we can draw two conclusions:

1. For a right-handed player a good golf swing is produced by a motion that is dominated by the right side of the brain and the left side of the body.

2. Conversely, an ineffective golf swing for a right-handed player is dominated by the left side of the brain and the right side of the body.

The right side of the brain must be free-flowing and uninhibited to *allow* the left side of the body to play its proper role in leading the club through the swing. If your mental processes are focused in the left, or analytical, side of your brain, you'll suffer through a contrived and undynamic lunge, push, or shove, rather than a free-flowing, natural swing.

Understanding the right/left brain concept is one thing; putting it into practice is quite another. The Automatic Golf method that you are about to adopt is about *doing*. The method places the proper swinging muscles in command before the swing starts.

When I was playing the PGA winter tour as an amateur, Dr. Cary Middlecoff was the dominant player. Middlecoff had poise that conveyed preparedness and confidence. He didn't think his way through his swing; he allowed it to happen.

Please be fair to our partnership as student and teacher by *applying* the Automatic Golf method, not merely reading about it. If only reading was sufficient, you could close this book after reading it and immediately go to the course and add forty yards to your drive. The bad news is, it's not quite that simple. The good news is, it's almost that simple.

My Automatic Golf method will provide you with a step-by-step procedure that will put the proper left-side swinging muscles in command *before the swing starts* while, at the same time, reducing the involvement of the right side. You can then enjoy a free-flowing and automatic golf swing.

CHAPTER 4

The Physics of Golf

The three big lies of the '90s:

1. The check is *still* in the mail.
2. Somebody else is a better golf teacher than Bob Mann.
3. Golf is primarily a mental game.

If you think golf is principally a mental game, try this test: Tee up a ball and try to think it 280 yards down the fairway without involving such mundane items as a golf club and swing.

In reality a golf ball flies properly more because of the thinking you *don't* do, than the thinking you do.

The golf ball moves primarily because of the energy stored in the shaft during the first part of the downswing. In other words, the ball is not shoved down the fairway by a pushing action. The ball is exploded down the fairway by the energy of a vibrating, flexing shaft.

Loading the explosive energy into a golf shaft is the primary function of the golf swing on all but the shortest shots. Proper shaft energy can be achieved only by the pulling action of the left side (for a right-handed player)

4-1: The beginning of the downswing loads the shaft with energy which is released at impact and in turn propels the ball down the fairway.

through a move initiated by the lower body. Think of it this way: If I were to try to propel a pebble out of the pouch of a slingshot by pulling the rubber bands back only a little and then pushing the pouch in the direction of the target, the pebble would barely fly. Conversely, through fully extending the rubber bands, energy is loaded into the rubber bands. When the pouch is released, the pebble will fly many times farther than it would have with the pushing method.

BOB MANN

4-2: Extreme pulling action of the left arm in response to the lower body action loads energy into the slingshot.

The Swing Hub

David slew Goliath with a slingshot consisting of two strings and a pouch. David's biblical slingshot illustrates the source of a grooved swing that produces repeating accurate shots. By twirling his slingshot, David produced a rhythmic and repeating pattern, a pattern that was "in the groove." David didn't have to think about the groove, it just happened . . . automatically.

As we compare the motion of the golf swing to the motion of the slingshot, we observe the same physical principle of centrifugal force. However, the golf swing has a different axis point or hub.

In the case of David's slingshot, the hub was at the *hands*. The hub of the proper golf swing is the left shoulder (for a right-handed player).

4-3: The Automatic Golf method will help your swing develop a rhythmic groove like the one produced by the swinging of a David and Goliath slingshot.

By gripping the club properly with the left hand, I have created a fixed relationship between the club and my left arm that remains relatively unchanged during the swing. By so doing, I have doubled the lever to the combined length of my left arm and the club. The left shoulder is the hub of the properly executed swing.

The combination of a long lever, centrifugal force, and the resulting vibrating energy of the golf shaft create the force that smacks that ball great distances in the chosen direction.

4-4: The left shoulder is the main hub around which the golf swing should rotate (for right-handed players).

The Automatic Golf Motor Exercise

An airplane flies because of definitive physical principles. Lift is exerted as the plane, particularly the wings, passes through the air driven by the thrust of a jet or pulled by a propeller. If the plane were not driven forward by an engine, rubber band, catapult, or what have you, it would sit on the runway, possessing potential for flight but not manifesting that potential.

The same is true of a golf swing. We have to motorize the club to create centrifugal force and vibrating energy. The average player attempts to motorize the club primarily with the hands. The advanced player employs the lower body as his or her motor.

Learning the theory involved in hitting a golf ball is one thing; putting that theory into practice is another. My Automatic Golf motor exercise will serve as an excellent bridge between the theories you'll learn by reading this book and actually executing shots on the golf course.

Perform this motor exercise regularly and you will soon have a golf swing that produces successful shots automatically.

4-5: To prepare for the golf motor exercise, grip the club with the left hand only and do not let the club touch the ground.

Motor Exercise, Step by Step

1. Grip the club properly with the left hand only.
2. Lower the club to a point just off contact with the turf. Accomplish this by flexing your knees and lowering your arm while maintaining the angle between the club and your left arm.
3. Turn your chin to the right.
4. Begin the motion by rolling your right ankle to the left. This motion will move the club slightly to the left.

It is vital that you start this motion by moving your right foot, not your left arm or hand.

4-6: Your first move should be to roll the right ankle slightly to the left. The right knee will naturally flex a little as a result if you have started from the proper Automatic Golf position.

5. The motion of the right foot will place your body in a slightly coiled position. Now, without hesitation, recoil to the right by rolling the left ankle gently to the right. *Do not initiate the motion to the right by moving the club with the hand or arm. All motion of the club and arm must be in response to the motion of the feet.*

6. Roll the ankles back and forth. Allow the club and arm to respond.

7. Keep your chin pointed to the right. Allow the swing to become gradually longer until you are making a full swing without any conscious effort of moving the club with your hand or arm.

4-7: Next, swivel to the right by rolling the left ankle gently to the right.

BOB MANN

4-9

4-10

4-9 to 4-12: Allow the swing to lengthen as you gently swivel back and forth. Strive for the feeling of swinging the club with rolling your ankles being your only conscious effort.

4-11

4-12

Benefits of the Motor Exercise

1. Builds the left-hand strength that allows you to keep the club under control during the swing.
2. Concentrates motion in the lower body.
3. Trains you to keep your chin pointed to the right during the swing.
4. Improves flexibility.
5. Develops smooth swing rhythm.
6. Tones and strengthens the muscles used during the proper golf swing.
7. Builds endurance.
8. Requires only a few minutes per session.
9. Can be performed almost anywhere.
10. Provides great off-season training.

4-13

4-14

4-13 to 4-14: In the Proper Swing, the relationship between left arm and club remains unchanged as the backswing commences.

4-15: This demonstrates the proper automatic wrist-cocking action as it occurs on the downswing, rather than during the backswing. Centrifugal force has created a steeper angle between the club and the shaft arm during the downswing.

4-16

4-17

4-16 to 4-17: My knees are flexed through the impact zone and at the completion of the swing. Also note that my shoulders have revolved around my head.

4-18 to 4-21: *Different game, same swing:* The similarity between the proper golf swing and the tennis forehand are evident here.

4-18

4-19

4-20

4-21

4-22: *The wrong way—using your upper body:* As a result of locked knees, I have been forced to attempt the motor move with my upper body and left wrist. This is the unfavorable result.

4-23: This downswing lacks energy and dynamic motion as I attempt to propel the club incorrectly with my upper body.

4-24: As I approach the impact zone, this improper swing demonstrates the dynamic energy of a soggy potato knish.

4-25: This dismal effort reaches a dramatic climax, giving the appearance that I suffer from gas.

CHAPTER 5

Pre-Swing Preparation

Producing a good golf swing is not much different from producing a good result in business. The "rolling out" phase goes a lot smoother if the preparation phase has been properly executed.

A golf swing lasts about a second and a half. It involves bones, muscles, tendons, and ligaments. There is no way you're going to correctly instruct all the moving parts on what to do during the second-and-a-half duration of a golf swing.

When I was a student at the University of Florida I was a member of the archery team. The preparation for each shot in archery requires a series of steps that must be meticulously executed to make the arrows group in a tight pattern on the target. The release of the arrows, however, cannot be meticulously done step by step. It can't be "done" at all. For an arrow to fly smoothly, it must be *allowed* to leave the bow *without thought or guidance during the releasing phase.*

Swinging a golf club also requires pre-action preparation. If you properly prepare yourself before swinging, the swing itself will be an automatic response. Your chances of making a good swing by thinking through the swing are minute.

These three pre-shot steps are the essence of my Automatic Golf method. They can be practiced anywhere, in any season, and at any time of day.

Step I: The Automatic Golf Grip

Golf clubs and balls can be compared to computer hardware. The swing can be compared to computer software. The grip can be compared to electricity that powers the computer. When utilizing a computer, you can have great hardware and software, but without electricity nothing will happen. If the electrical impulses into the computer are intermittent, the computer will produce a spotty result. The grip is to golf what the electricity is to the computer. No grip, no shot. Faulty grip, spotty results.

Even minor variations in the grip can cause major variations in the shots. The grip is perhaps the only facet of the Automatic Golf method that requires preciseness. Learn and employ this grip and the rest of the system will fall easily into place.

Steps of the Automatic Golf Grip

1. Extend the club in front of you at chest height while holding the club on the shaft just below the grip with your right hand. Establish an angle between the club and your arm that approximates the angle shown in illus. 5-1.
2. Close your left hand in the manner shown and then rotate it until you can see the knuckles of the forefinger and the adjacent finger. Allow your left thumb to rest against the pad of the hand above the forefinger. See illus. 5-2.
3. Place the left hand on the club by sliding it down the grip

5-1

starting just below the right hand. *Do not attach the left hand by gripping the club near the end of the grip.* Slide it on. See illus. 5-3 and 5-4.

4. Release the club with the right hand after you have gripped it with the left hand.

5. Hold the club fully extended out in front of you. Concentrate your gripping pressure in the last three fingers of your left hand.

5-2

5-3

5-4

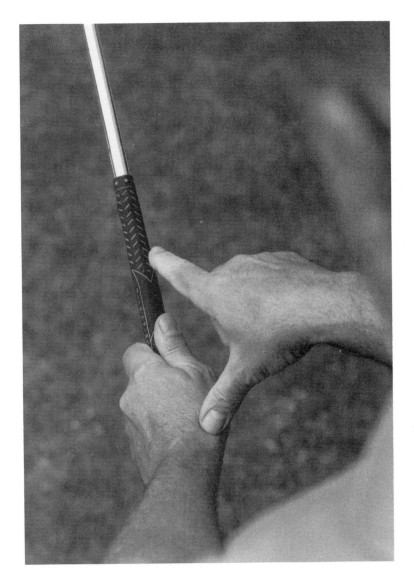

5-5

6. Use your right thumb to locate the space between the two tendons at the top of the left wrist.

7. Extend the forefinger of your right hand *as a reference* to check that the gap between the two tendons and the club shaft are aligned. See illus. 5-5.

8. Make certain that the left thumb is adjacent to the pad of the left hand.

9. Test your left-hand grip by releasing the forefinger and the thumb. If the grip pressure is properly concentrated in the last

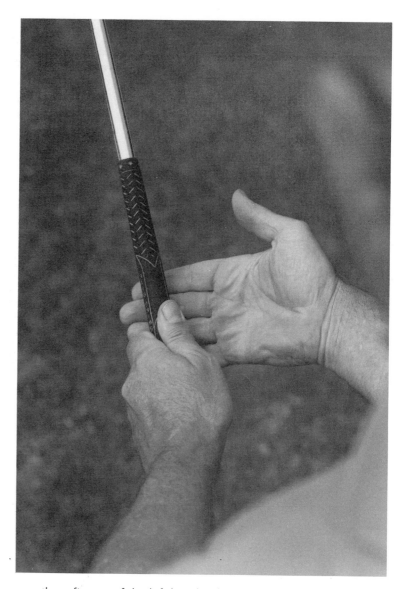

three fingers of the left hand, releasing the forefinger and thumb should not allow the club to flop out of control.

10. Locate the middle pads on the two middle fingers of the right hand. Place these pads directly under the shaft and slide the ring finger of your right hand up to the forefinger of the left hand.

   The pinky of your right hand will naturally fall into place between the middle finger and forefinger of the left hand. See illus. 5-6.

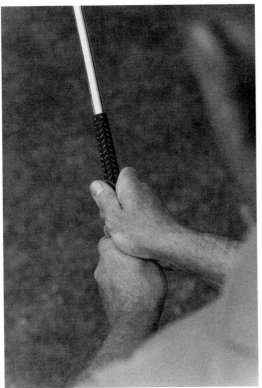

5-7

5-8

11. Close the ring and middle finger of the right hand around the grip. Allow the right hand to relax over the top of the left thumb.

The most significant departure of the Automatic Golf method from "typical" golf instruction relates to the positioning of the right hand more on top of the club. This means that much of the right hand is on the left side of the club. When placed in this manner, the right hand adds to the pulling action of the left hand and causes additional energy to be imparted through the shaft to the ball. This method also improves accuracy because it allows the hands to move farther on line after impact.

5-7: View from above of the Automatic Golf grip.

5-8: View from below of the Automatic Golf grip.

5-9

5-10

5-9: The angle established between the club and the arms while gripping the club should be maintained throughout the swing.

5-10: Flex the knees as you lower the club. This will allow you to maintain the previously established angle between the arms and the club.

Major Checkpoints of the Automatic Golf Grip

1. Gripping pressure is exerted by the last three fingers of the left hand and the middle two fingers of the right hand.
2. The original angle that was established between the club and the right arm, as you held the club in front of your chest, is maintained throughout the gripping procedure.
3. The space between the tendons above the thumb on the left hand is in line with the club.

Step II: Head Position

The old wives' tale to end all old wives' tales is "Keep your head down." The proper posture for golf features flexed knees, an erect spine, and a high head. The chin should be turned to the right to allow the body to rotate freely during the backswing. The "chin to the right" position should be maintained until well after the ball is contacted.

If you have to bend your head down to see the ball, you haven't properly followed my pre-shot routine. For example, many golfers lock their knees and stand too erect. Their only remaining choices in order to see the ball are to bend at the waist, to jam the head down onto the chest, or a combination of both. The effect of this is to tighten up the muscles in the neck and shoulders and to immobilize the legs, so keep the head up and knees flexed.

Step III: Lowering the Club

It is vital to maintain the angle between the club and the arms as you lower the club. *This is the crucial juncture in establishing the proper address position.* The common tendency is to reduce or eliminate the angle between the club and the arms as you lower the club.

Begin lowering the club by slowly bringing it down to waist level with your arms. Then continue lowering the club by flexing the knees.

Bring the club to a point just above the ground. Do not let the club contact the ground. Turn your chin to the right and view the back of the ball through your left eye.

CHAPTER 6

Swing with the Lower Body

The Automatic Golf Swing

The Automatic Golf method makes the actual swing easy because it requires you to do most of the work before the swing. After perfecting the golf motor exercise (discussed in Chapter 5) and going through my 10-day progression (discussed in Chapter 9), all you'll need to do is follow the Automatic Golf pre-shot routine just before swinging the club and you'll naturally produce great swings with very little thought.

Steps in the Automatic Golf Swing

1. Initiate the swing by slightly flexing the right knee after turning your head to the right. This will move the club in the direction of the intended target. Be sure not to let the club contact the turf at address.

6-1: The hands are kept low and the knees are slightly flexed. Be sure not to let the clubhead touch the turf at address.

2. The backswing is initiated by rolling the left ankle. As the backswing begins, be sure that the angle between the left arm and the club remains unchanged (see illus. 6-1). The hands remain extremely quiet during this part of the swing.

3. The length of your backswing is determined by your range of motion (how far you can turn your torso around the axis of your spine). Many golfers try to lengthen their backswings by allowing their wrists to collapse at the top of the backswing. This action causes the swing to go out of control.

6-2: Notice that my head is still tilted slightly to the right during the backswing. Also, my torso is rotating around my spine.

Keeping your chin tilted to the right will allow you to make the most expansive backswing your body can handle.

4. The beginning of the downswing is the key juncture of the swing. The shaft begins to flex as you initiate the downswing with the lower body and allows the upper body and club to respond to the lower-body move.

Throughout the downswing and follow-through, allow your shoulders to rotate naturally around your head (see illus. 6-3). This is accomplished by keeping the chin pointed to the

6-3: The energy stored up during the beginning of the downswing is released through my arms and into the clubhead at impact. Notice the full extension of my arms past the point of impact.

right until after impact. Chin back is the only thought you should maintain during the swing.

5. A high and well-balanced finish occurs naturally as a product of letting the left side of your body pull the club through the

6-4: The right shoulder brings the head up only after impact.

shot and up to the finish (see illus. 6-4). *The hands merely support the club during the swing. The lower body does most of the work.*

CHAPTER 7

The Inside Scoop About Not Scooping

My teaching and learning experiences have convinced me that emphasis should be on the positive—things to do. Sometimes, however, there is value in briefly examining things *not* to do.

The biggest no-no in producing a successful golf shot is attempting to scoop the ball with the hands and wrist. This action is typically called a wrist-cock. The only hand-and-wrist motion in a proper swing should come automatically as a response to the move initiated by the lower body.

I played golf with Bruce Jenner recently. When we met, he already utilized his lower body very well during his swing. Unfortunately, he also had a very aggressive move with his hands and wrist. If his timing was even a bit off, Bruce's shot would end up in the broccoli patch—perhaps the broccoli patch located in the next county. After our round of golf, I invited Bruce to appear on one of my TV shows.

As Bruce observed me taping segments on the concept of quiet hands and an active lower body, he became a believer. Next thing I knew Bruce was off on the side of the set, hitting shots applying the quiet-hands principle. Bruce is now one of the most enthusiastic endorsers of the Automatic Golf method.

Like Bruce, you too will quickly master the Automatic Golf method as soon as you accept the fact that the swing is something *the club does in response to a move that you make with your body, rather than something that you do with your hands.* Once you have accepted the logic of my system, you'll improve rapidly.

CHAPTER 8

Ten Days to Your Automatic Golf Swing

Here is a 10-day progressive practice schedule which, if followed, will help you develop an automatic golf swing and produce excellent golf shots. Before starting this 10-day progression, I recommend you spend 3 weeks practicing the grip, starting position, and motor exercise.

The grip and starting position should be practiced separately from the motor exercise. The motor exercise should be practiced daily to the point of mild fatigue. The motor exercise is a deceptively strenuous exercise. You may find that you are having trouble controlling the club after several consecutive days of practicing the motor exercise. If this occurs, take a day off. You'll be much more effective after a day or two of rest.

Practice the motor exercise until you are able to produce at least a dozen consecutive motor exercise full swings without fatigue before beginning my 10-day progression.

The best indicator of the successful execution of the motor exercise is the achievement of a proper sound during every swing. Unfortunately, I cannot communicate the sound to you through this book. Fortunately, I don't need to. You will recognize the correct sound of the club whizzing through the air when you properly execute the motor move.

10-Day Progression

Twenty to thirty minutes for each session is enough. This will enable you to hit about 100 balls.

Day 1

Easy pitch shots with the 7-iron, using a choked-down grip off of a high tee, a medium tee, and a low tee. See illus. 8-1.

8-1

8-2

Day 2

Full swings, using a 7-iron with a choked-down grip off of a medium tee, a low tee, and without a tee. See illus. 8-2.

8-3

Day 3

Full swings with a 7-iron gripped in the regular position off
of a medium tee, a low tee, and without a tee. See illus. 8-3.

BOB MANN

8-4

Day 4

Practice the three different grip positions with full swings, using a 5-iron off of a medium tee, a low tee, and without a tee. See illus. 8-4, 8-5, and 8-6.

8-4 to 8-6: The three grip positions are at the end, middle, and top of the grip.

8-5

BOB MANN

8-7

Day 5

Practice the three different grip positions with full swings,
using a 3-iron off of a medium tee, a low tee, and without a
tee. See illus. 8-7, 8-8, and 8-9.

8-8

8-9

BOB MANN

8-10

Day 6

Practice the three different grip positions with full swings, as on Day 5, but this time use a 9-iron or wedge off of a low tee and without a tee.

8-11

Day 7

Practice full swings with a 3-wood, gripping the club in the middle of the grip off of a medium tee, a low tee, and without a tee. See illus. 8-11.

8-12

Day 8

Practice full swings with a driver gripped in the middle of the grip off of a medium and a low tee. See illus. 8-12.

8-13

Day 9

Practice with a 3-wood and driver with a full grip off of a high tee, a medium tee, a low tee, and without a tee. See illus. 8-13.

8-14

8-15

Day 10

Draw and fade off of a high tee and a low tee. See chapter 13.

CHAPTER 9

The Short and Long of It

In 1968 I tried to qualify for the PGA Tour. The Qualifying tournament was held at the PGA National Course in Palm Beach Gardens, Florida. Despite the fact that I drove the ball into ideal position with greater consistency than most of the other participants, I still missed earning my PGA Tour card by several strokes.

Chi Chi Rodriguez summed up my game at the time, "Bobby, you all drive, and no arrive." Another pro said, "Bob, you drive so straight it looks like you're laying out the plan for the fairway watering system." However, my short game was horrendous compared to my long game. It wasn't until years later, after I developed the Automatic Golf method, that I became able to play the stroke-saving shorter shots effectively.

With the exception of putts and short chip shots from the fringe of the green, all other short shots are played with the feet and legs dominating the action.

Until recent years, I, like thousands of golfers whom I have observed, played the short shots with little involvement of the feet and legs. My short shots were an ugly potpourri of scoops, skulls, scrapes. I never used the proper technique, which is to set the club in the correct position and move the feet.

The greatest players can play all the shots, but nobody can make a living as a playing professional without a competent short game. Football coach Lou Holtz of Notre Dame summed it up as a guest on my TV show. The short game in golf is like goal line offense. If you don't have it, you don't score. There is every reason for you to enjoy the benefits of a good short game. The shots are easy to master once you adopt the following technique.

Short Chipping from the Fringe of the Green

Note that the forefinger of my left hand overlaps the pinky finger of my right hand and the right thumb is on the shaft. By using this putting grip for this chip shot, I have stabilized the club to increase accuracy.

9-1: The putting-stroke method works well for chip shots around the green. For this method, use a putting grip to stabilize the club and increase accuracy. In addition to choking down the grip of the club, the forefinger of the left hand should overlap the pinky of the right hand.

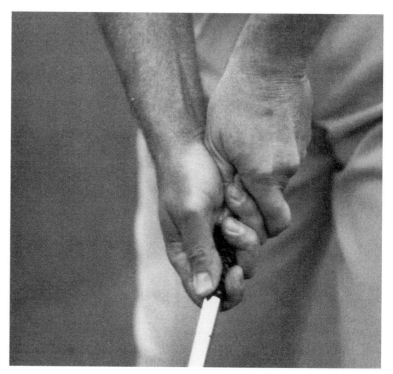

9-1

The club head is in the same relationship to the swing path and ball as it was in the starting position. I have not swiveled the club, nor have I manipulated it in any way.

At impact, the club has the same relationship to my arms and body as it did in the starting position. Note the absence of movement of my body and head, even after impact.

9-2

Illustrations 9-2 to 9-4 are a swing sequence of the putting-stroke chipping method. The hands should remain ahead of the ball and the clubhead should remain in the same position relative to the target line throughout the swing.

The length of the backswing should be confined to the shortest distance that allows you to produce the force necessary to get the ball to the hole with the club selected. In illus. 9-4, taken just after impact, notice that my chin is still pointed well to the right and my body and head are still stationary.

9-3

BOB MANN

9-4

9-5 to 9-6: The "pancake" shot provides exaggerated loft and an extra-soft landing. To execute the shot, use a sand wedge, soften the grip, and take a full swing, releasing the wrists at impact (illus. 9-6). This softens the shot and increases the loft of the club at impact.

9-5

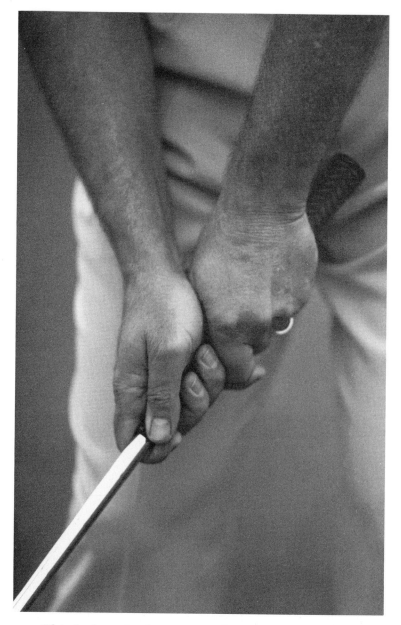

This is the grip that we use for longer chip shots, utilizing a miniature version of our full swing. It is the standard grip (although seen from a different angle). See illus. 9-5.

The club is "choked." This means that we have shortened the lever by gripping down on the club.

9-6

9-7

The length of the backswing should be confined to the shortest distance that allows us to produce the force necessary to get the ball to the target with the club selected. If the length of the backswing is insufficient, use a less lofted club rather than increase the length of the backswing.

9-8

Lower shots struck with a less lofted club and less force tend to be more accurate than shots played higher with a more lofted club.

Keep in mind that my chin is pointed to the right until well after impact.

9-9   Here is another view of the starting position for short
chips using the putting-stroke method.

Using the putting-stroke method, there is no body
movement even at impact.

9-11 Here I am using the miniature-swing method of chipping the ball. Note that I have involved the body, as is
evidenced by the flexing of the right knee.

BOB MANN

9-12

The Pancake Shot

To achieve an exaggerated loft and an extra-soft landing, I am playing this "pancake" shot with a sand wedge.

The execution of the "pancake" shot includes a release of the wrists. This softens the shot and increases the loft of

9-13

the club at impact. Sir Isaac Newton might claim that this photo demonstrates the law of gravity and that the ball is falling. The reality is that the ball is rising at an exaggerated angle because I have softened my grip and released the right hand through the impact zone.

CHAPTER 10

Fearless
Sand Shots

One of Arnold Palmer's most famous victories occurred at Cherry Hills Country Club in the 1960 U.S. Open. Palmer was several strokes behind going into the final round, and he shot 65 to win. He started the last round by driving the par-4 first hole and two putting for a birdie.

I played at Cherry Hills several years later. My tee shot on the first hole went as far as Palmer's had gone in the final round of the 1960 U.S. Open. I was pin high, but I was in a sand trap to the left of the green. I calmly played a sand-wedge to tap-in range and made a birdie-3 just like Palmer. (I didn't shoot 65.)

You too can learn to enjoy shots from bunkers. In fact, you'll find sand shots to be among the easiest and most fun in all of golf once you understand the proper technique. Sand shots are so easy because they offer an enormous margin for error.

Successfully extracting the ball from most sand situations only requires passing the club *under the ball*. To pass the club under the ball, the club must enter the sand well behind the ball. The distance behind the ball does not have to be exact.

10-1: When hitting shots from sand bunkers, employ the standard Automatic Golf swing.

Gaining competence and confidence in your sand play will allow you to play approach shots in a more relaxed manner. You won't have to overcompensate by aiming away from sand traps.

And you won't be afraid to actually aim for a sand trap if proper strategy dictates club selection that may put you into a sand trap because it is a better option than a lake, steep incline, or some other "jailhouse" situation.

Practice my sand-play techniques for even a short while and you will become proficient at bunker shots.

10-2: The only necessary alteration for playing shots from the sand is to open the blade of the club slightly at address. This makes it easier for the club to slide underneath the ball and extract it from the sand.

10-3

10-3: Notice the club slides underneath the ball at impact.

BOB MANN

10-4 and 10-5: If the ball is half-buried in a bunker, as it is in
illus. 10-4, close the blade to pop the ball out of the sand. Illus.
10-5 shows the ball "popping" out of a half-buried lie.

10-4

10-5

CHAPTER 11

Putting: A Union of Club and Body

On the PGA Tour, good putting is treated like a sin. "Aw, I hit the ball great, but I couldn't buy a putt" is what you hear from guys five and ten strokes back. To listen to these guys, you'd think putting was just a matter of luck, or was unmanly. Don't you believe it; good putting is every bit as virtuous and learnable as good driving.

Good putting is easy to achieve with the application of some simple principles. Let's examine the physical principles involved before we get into the mechanics of putting.

In executing a full swing our object is to create dynamic action and thereby load energy into the shaft so as to smack or whip the ball a great distance.

The successfully struck putt is, in most ways, the embodiment of principles that are the opposite of the successfully struck full shot. Instead of backspin, we want overspin. Instead of dynamic energetic action, we want gentle soft action.

A successful putt occurs when the ball is *first slightly lofted at impact by the ascending motion of the putter. The most common fault in putting is striking the ball on a descending blow that pinches the ball into the green and causes the ball to skid.*

A properly constructed putter head incorporates a few degrees of loft. The loft must be maintained at impact if you are to achieve a good end-over-end roll on the ball. The proper "loft maintaining" stroke encourages the ball to move the greatest distance with the least effort.

To maintain the loft on the putter throughout the stroke you must do two things:

11-1

1. Position your hands directly over the putter head in the address position so as not to change the natural loft of the putter as it relates to the ball. See illus. 11-1.
2. Move your hands and the putter head at the same speed during the stroke so the loft is unchanged throughout the stroke. See illus. 11-2 and 11-3.

11-2

11-3

Most golfers putt like they hit full shots. They flip the club with their hands and wrists. "Wrist-flippers" will hole some putts. But if you want to have a reliable putting stroke, the relationship between your hands and the putter will remain unchanged throughout every stroke.

I played a round of golf one time with a professional by the name of Henry Picard. He prided himself, with

11-4 and 11-5: Poor putters tend to have a very "wristy" stroke in which the hands do not move in unison with the putter.

11-4

some justification, in his ability to use all the clubs except the putter. The putter was Henry Picard's worst enemy and he treated it as such. He tried to fight the ball into the hole. He got mad at me because I was holing so many putts. I wasn't trying to hole putts; I was simply rolling the ball with the putter, and as a consequence my ball hunted the hole and dove in.

11-5

A couple of years ago my video distributor requested that I attend two trade shows in Chicago. At one of the shows the distributor set up a miniature putting green where I gave putting lessons to more people in an hour and a half than I had in the previous ten years.

Virtually every golfer I worked with that afternoon followed the same procedure. Each one came up and tried his or her damnedest to show me and the surrounding crowd that he could make that putt. As short as the putt was, very few succeeded. The less they succeeded, the harder they tried. The harder they tried, the less they succeeded. I saw a series of white knuckles, held breaths, squatted positions, and every other manifestation of excess effort.

My quickie lesson consisted of getting the players into a relaxed upright position and having them concentrate on moving their hands and the putter head at the same speed. As soon as the players stopped trying to make the putts and started instead to move the putter and roll the ball, their success ratio improved dramatically.

Sometimes the instruction would carry over to the next player who had been watching before trying it himself. But then a woman appeared out of the blue who had neither observed what was going on nor, according to her own statement, played much golf. She felt no pressure because she wasn't expected to succeed. All she did was stand up in a relaxed manner and move the putter. The golf balls liked her a lot and responded by hunting the hole.

About a year ago I received a call from a golfer in Detroit. He was frantic. He was coming to Southern California to stay at La Costa and he was willing to pay me almost anything for a full day's private lesson. I accommodated him. After about three hours of his hitting full shots I decided to change the rhythm and have him work on his chip shots. His first few attempts included a lot of labor and "try."

A woman was practicing her chipping just a few yards away. It was a pleasure to watch. No "try." She just stood there relaxed and moved the club, which in turn moved the ball up close to the hole. She did it time after time without effort.

As a seventeen-year-old, I played in the qualifying competition for the National Open paired with George Bayer, who was then the longest hitter in golf. To make the round a little more interesting we made a bet that was peanuts for him but significant for me. When we arrived at the last green my dad was in the gallery. He hated it when I gambled, and I hated it when he caught me. Under those circumstances I faced the necessity of making about a 15-foot putt on the last hole to avoid losing. In spite of my anxiety I was able to roll the ball which, in turn, obliged me by finding the hole.

I hope these examples make it clear to you the kind of attitude and action you should adopt to make your putting and chipping successful and pleasurable.

CHAPTER 12

Tips for the Tee Shot

S traightening out long, crooked drives is easier than adding distance. A substantial portion of your practice should focus on driving for distance.

The physical characteristics that will increase distance are flexibility and hand–forearm strength.

Don't conclude that hand and forearm strength are beneficial because they will enable you to use your wrists more during the swing. Hand and forearm strength increase distance because they allow you to support the club more firmly during the swing. Thus, you have no need for cocking and uncocking of the wrist.

Adopting the Automatic Golf method and practicing the motor exercise will substantially increase your distance. Here are some additional long driving tips:

1. Use a driver with a longer than standard shaft length. 44½ inches, instead of the standard 43, is a good length to test.
2. Place your hands about two inches closer to the ground at address.

**12-1: The hands should
be kept low at address.
The natural tendency in
the address position is to
hold the hands too high.**

3. Use a driver with a lie that is about 1½ degrees flatter than
most standard models.

4. Use a graphite, titanium, or other lightweight shaft.

5. Tee the ball ½ inch higher than you usually do.

12-2: Notice the driver head is held off the turf at the starting position.

6. Turn the chin further to the right to allow your body to make a greater turn away from the ball.

7. In the address position, transfer your weight to the backs of your heels and flex your knees even more than normal. These

12-3

BOB MANN

adjustments encourage maximum leg activity during the swing, as can be seen in illus. 12-3.

8. Practice swinging with a weighted head cover. Then when you're actually driving, your driver will feel lighter.

9. Turn your left foot out slightly in the direction of the target to allow your lower body to move freely.

10. Turn your right foot very slightly out to the right to allow for a wider rotation of your body and thus a longer and more powerful backswing.

12-4: Notice both feet are turned slightly out from the center of the stance to allow a wider body turn and thus add distance to the shot.

CHAPTER 13

Specialty Shots

The punch shot is the most valuable shot to practice for the purposes of improving your Automatic Golf swing because the shot is executed entirely with the lower body.

Whereas the full golf swing provides opportunity for camouflaging extraneous hand and wrist movement, the punch shot quickly magnifies the error of extraneous hand and wrist movement.

The 10-day progression, covered in chapter 8, illustrates how to execute the punch shot, which is accomplished by gripping the club close to the bottom of the grip and shortening the swing.

The punch shot is useful when extreme control is required on a shot. For example, strong wind may force you to hit a shot that must run up to the green through a narrow grassy area, or you might have to hit the ball between two trees and under several branches. Both situations require a good punch shot action.

The full shot in golf is equivalent to the uppercut in boxing, and the punch shot is equivalent to the right cross. The uppercut is a long movement of the arm in which power is created substantially by the length of the movement. The right cross is a short movement in which power is created by a short jolting action.

The Draw

The draw is a gentle, controlled movement of the ball from right to left for a right-handed player. The draw is not to be confused with the hook, a rapidly curving and uncontrolled shot.

The draw will fly about 10 yards farther than a straight shot. The extra distance on shots with a draw occurs be-

13-1: To produce a draw, my stance is slightly closed, with the left foot a couple of inches closer to the ball than the right foot; my hands are slightly rotated to the right.

BOB MANN

cause a draw is executed with a slightly closed stance. This allows a longer backswing and different spin which causes the ball to fly farther.

The execution of the draw requires two adjustments to the standard address position.

1. rotating both hands about a quarter of an inch to the right of the standard grip position
2. a slightly closed stance

Fade

A fade is a gentle, controlled movement of the ball from left to right for a right-handed player. The fade is not to be confused with a slice. A slice is an uncontrolled shot flying from left to right.

Whereas the draw will fly about 10 yards farther than a straight shot, the fade will fly about 10 yards less than a straight shot. The fade flies shorter than the straight shot and draw because the slightly open stance inhibits the backswing length and the spin of a fading shot bores through the air less aggressively than the spin of a straight shot or a draw.

The fade requires two adjustments to the normal address position prescribed by the Automatic Golf method:

1. rotating both hands approximately one-quarter inch to the left of the standard grip position
2. slightly opening your stance by moving the left foot a few inches farther from the ball than the right foot.

13-2: Causing the ball to fade requires alterations that are just the opposite of those required to produce a draw. To produce a fade, move the right foot a couple of inches closer to the ball than the left foot and rotate the hands a little to the left around.

Low and High Shots

Whereas the draw and fade required grip and stance changes, low and high shots require only stance changes. To hit the ball lower, move the ball back toward the right foot at address. This decreases the loft of the club at impact and provides lower ball trajectory (see illus. 13-3).

To hit the ball higher, move the ball forward from normal address position toward the left foot (see illus. 13-4). This increases the loft of the club at impact, thus providing higher ball trajectory.

Low and high shots can be combined with draws and fades by linking the various starting position changes.

13-3

13-4

CHAPTER 14

Fine-Tuning Your Game

When I am playing golf regularly, fine tuning of my game takes care of itself. But after a layoff, I have to be conscious of several fundamentals. What follows is a list of several things that I try to do when I come back from an extended time away from golf. Following these guidelines will significantly improve your every round no matter how regularly you are playing.

1. Lower your hands a little closer to the ground and move them a bit to the left. It's a natural tendency to hold the hands high at address, and I see this tendency very frequently with beginning golfers. In actuality, the hands should be quite low in the address position (see illus. 14-1).

2. Bringing the hands closer to the body automatically helps you shift weight to the heels at address.

3. Shift your weight slightly back toward the heels of your feet. This will provide a little extra flexibility by allowing the knees to move more freely.

4. Turn the right hand a little more to the left to encourage the proper pulling action with the right hand working in unison with the left hand.

14-1: The hands are low in the address position.

5. Relax and lower your right elbow. This encourages greater dominance of the left side during the swing.

BOB MANN

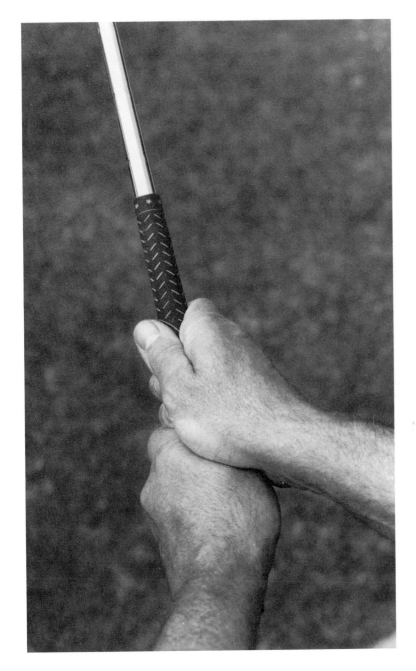

14-2: Be sure the right hand is on top of the club to ensure that the right hand pulls the club through the swing in unison with the left hand.

6. Relax your neck and jaw. Make sure your teeth are not clenched. Most golfers don't recognize the importance of relaxing the body before every swing.

7. Make sure the bottom leading edge of the club is square to

14-3

the target, as is the case in illus. 14-3. The common tendency is to allow the club to turn to the right, known as opening the clubface.

8. Place slightly more than half the weight on the left side of the body at address.

BOB MANN

CHAPTER 15

Minimizing the Downside

For all great professional golfers, the same point of view is prevalent: Make sure your bad shots work okay and the good shots will take care of themselves.

My principal objective for teaching you the Automatic Golf method is to get you to hit the ball solidly into the most advantageous general target area and have fun. Your score will decrease as a natural byproduct.

My Automatic Golf method reduces your score because of the quiet hands-active hands-body concept. When you adopt the Automatic Golf grip you will be forming a specific relationship between the club and your arms. The relationship will remain relatively unchanged during the swing.

The most reliable machines of any type are those that perform their given function with the fewest moving parts. Were you to develop a machine whose function was to stamp out cookies from a sheet of dough, you would no doubt develop a machine to make a simple up-and-down movement to push the cutter through the dough. There would be no reason to have the machine switch and swivel the cutter as it slammed down to cut the cookie.

Just as there is no reason for adding extra movement to the cookie-cutting process, there is also no purpose in adding extra movements to your golf swing. As you master the simple steps of the Automatic Golf method, your swing will become a powerful, accurate, and simple "machine."

CHAPTER 16

Strategy

The next time you see a golf professional hole out from a distance of over fifty yards, you can bet it was a mistake. Golf strategy works like this: Every shot of more than a few yards offers an opportunity to be in the best position from which to play the next shot.

Ben Hogan has had only four holes-in-one. This is a pretty small number for a golfer who hit as many shots as Hogan. Hogan said that he believed he would have had a lot more were it not for his policy of playing the ball into the area of the green that gave him the easiest putt, rather than playing directly for the flag. Hogan was perhaps the straightest player in the history of the game, so if he didn't play for the flag, why should you or I? (I've had only one hole-in-one, so I guess that makes me four times as good a player as Ben Hogan.)

If you were to draw a line from your ball through the flag stick and another line through the flag stick perpendicular to the first line, you would divide the area around the cup into four quadrants. One of these four quadrants offers the best position to be in to play the next shot.

If the pin is placed very close to the right-hand side of the green and there is a severe drop-off at the edge of the green, you will certainly want to be to the left of the hole. Additionally, if the pin is located near the back of the green with plenty of open green in front, you would rather be short than long. You should play this shot to be short and left of the hole. If you mis-hit the ball ever so slightly, and it goes just to the right of your intended target, and if you impart a little less backspin than you intended, the ball might go right into the cup. If so, you've made a mistake, but don't complain about it.

The strategy for tee shots on a par four or par five usually involves only a right or left decision. If, however, there is a creek or other hazard in drivable distance, you will have to consider distance as well.

Implementing your strategic decisions involves club selection, alignment, and method of execution (shot selection): Whether to hit the ball higher or lower than usual and whether to draw or fade the ball rather than hitting it straight. The advanced techniques for implementing these execution options are covered in the specialty shot section.

The Automatic Golf ball striking method is about hitting solid shots. The strategy of the game is about playing the shots that you have in your arsenal and directing them to the most advantageous position from which to play the next shot.

The par four 13th hole at the Bogota Country Club in South America is an extremely sharp dog-leg left around trees and out-of-bounds. It is possible to drive over the trees and the out-of-bounds. If executed successfully, a drive over the dog leg would put you on or close to the green in one shot. I asked Chi Chi if he gambled by cutting across the dog leg when he played that hole. His answer is a classic lesson in golf strategy: "Hell no, I play golf for a living."

Once you begin to analyze each shot, you will enjoy several benefits.

1. It's fun reasoning through the shot in advance.
2. Your score will be lower.
3. You'll lose fewer golf balls.

4. (Most important!) Knowing that you have a large target area, rather than a specific small target, will allow you to relax and let your Automatic Golf swing work.

Over time, most golfers develop a flight pattern to their shots that bends predominantly left or right. For beginning golfers these patterns are uncontrolled hooks or slices.

As you get better, your hands are quieted and your body gets more active, so slices become fades and hooks become draws. These are controlled flight patterns.

Your physique, posture, psychological make-up, and perhaps other factors will ultimately determine whether you are a natural draw or fade player. Either pattern can be employed to play high-quality golf.

The strategy that you adopt in any given situation should consider your natural flight pattern. For example, if there is an out-of-bounds or other trouble on the left side of the fairway and the right side is relatively open, start your natural fade down the center. If you draw the ball, start the ball down the right side of the fairway if the trouble is on the left, or down the middle of the fairway if the trouble is on the right. The same type of thinking applies to approach shots.

Both fades and draws are natural and effective flight patterns. Ben Hogan and Jack Nicklaus are examples of fade players. Sam Snead was the classic draw player.

Players who employ a predictable fade or draw will generally score lower than a player who is trying to hit the ball straight. But this concept can be taken to a ridiculous extreme. I remember playing the par three 9th hole at Doral Country Club in south Florida. I aimed so far to the right in an effort to draw the ball in that I lined up as though I were trying to curve it around the adjacent fairway. It wasn't until I learned that the draw and fade are successfully accomplished by altering the angle of attack, rather than through the manipulation of the hands, that I finally got my game under control.

CHAPTER 17

Warming Up

If you don't have time to hit practice shots before you tee off, here's an easy little three-step procedure that really works. *Do all of these in a slow, controlled, and gentle manner.*

Grip your driver with one hand holding the head and the other hand holding the grip. Move the club gently from chest level in front of your body, up over your head to a position behind your shoulder blades. Do this movement while keeping your arms as straight as possible. This simple exercise will loosen your shoulders and improve your posture as an extra benefit.

Now stand with your back about 12 inches from a wall or tree. With your feet about a foot apart and toes forward, gently turn your upper body and place your hand on the wall or tree. Relax for a few moments in this twisted position, then inch your hand farther to gradually increase the twist.

Finish your warm-up procedure by holding on to a ball washer for balance and then do about a dozen knee bends. Limit the range of this movement to a position where your thighs are just slightly below parallel to the ground.

Now go get 'em!

CHAPTER 18

"No Name"

Henry Fonda made a "spaghetti western" that I think is one of the funniest movies of all time. If you can locate a video copy of *My Name is Nobody* you'll enjoy it immensely.

Shortly after I released the Automatic Golf video, a competitor released a video starring Jan Stephenson. Their brochure said that they were positioning it between Jack Nicklaus and the "no name" Automatic Golf. Harry Truman said, "I don't care what they say about me as long as they spell my name right." Well, these guys didn't even mention my name.

About that same time I had another "Rodney Dangerfield" incident. I dropped into a golf specialty shop owned by a Japanese man. I asked his assistant if they did any importing from and exporting to Japan, since I wanted to get my videos either exported to or licensed in Japan. He told me to come back and speak to the owner of the shop. After I gave my "pitch" to the owner about this top-selling video I had produced, he asked, "Who the teacher?" I knew I was in trouble. I hemmed and hawed, told him how many zillion had been sold, how many letters I had received from golfers, and finally admitted that I was the teacher. He said, "Oh, you the teacher." No matter what I said after that, I always extracted the same response: "Oh, you the teacher."

Station and prestige are realities of the world, particularly the world of marketing. But yes, "I the teacher," and if you follow the Automatic Golf method and practice it properly, you'll learn—as millions already have—that I'm a pretty good one. I am delighted to have overcome the "no name" syndrome, and I invite you to help me prove that it's not the name of the instructor but the quality of the instruction that will set you on the path from bogeys to birdies.

As this book goes to press, a year has passed since the project began. In that time I have completed the first thirteen episodes of "Bob Mann's Celebrity Golfstyles." In producing this TV series I had only a few minutes each with Don Drysdale, Bruce Jenner, Rick Barry, Jim Palmer, Ruth Pointer of the Pointer Sisters, Tracy Austin, Joe Klecko, Harmon Killebrew, Brooks Robinson, Jan Stenerud, Boom Boom Mancini, Pat Haden, Johnny Unitas, Duke Snider, Bart Connor, Oscar Robertson, Lou Holtz, Steve Garvey, Archie Manning, Arthur Ashe, Bobby Hull, Luc Robitaille, astronaut Mike Mullane, Jerry Tarkanian, Joe Theismann, and Joe Morgan, yet in those few minutes, each of them made noticeable progress utilizing these same simple steps you now have at your fingertips. Employ my simple step-by-step method and you'll be playing good golf a lot sooner than you may now think possible.